Congrats on your
kick ass journey!
Love. Mo.

what if ...

The World is
All for You?

VMH™ Publishing
Atlanta, GA

what if ...

The World is
All for You?

Created and Written by: Maureen "Mo" Faul

Illustrations by: Laura Nielsen

VMH™ Publishing
3355 Lenox Rd. NE Ste 750
Atlanta, GA 30326
vmhpublishing.com

The publisher is not responsible for websites, or social media pages (or their content) related to this publication, that are not owned by the publisher. Quantity sales. Special discounts are available on quantity purchases by corporations, associations, and others. For details, contact the publisher via email at: info@vmhpublishing.com

LCCN: 2021908963

Hardback ISBN: 978-1-947928-97-8

Published in United States of America

10 9 8 7 6 5 4 3 2 1

Introduction

Once upon a time, an ambitious woman struggled to be who she was supposed to be. The world was hard and the climb of life was steep. My career and soul spent way too many years separated. I wondered if I would ever find peace inside me. Then, one day, the doctors said, "cancer" and my world was turned upside down.

I was introduced to my soul in a new way as I became acquainted with my vulnerability, over and over again. My body suffered many physical challenges; at times all I could rely on was my soul. The inner self had to take over. Through this adversity, I found a new sense of self, which I share often with my audience and those who stumble upon my work.

Last year, a pandemic swept the world. The energy of change that was all about us initiated another period of deep reflection for me as I scurried about, like a squirrel in early winter, to collect and store as many lovely lives and souls who needed help and lifting as I could.

The world is changed forever. It's never been clearer that we need each other. We need our soul. Our soul is what directs our lives. Our soul is the very truth and energy we need to live a fulfilled life. Read on and enjoy.

Love, Mo

What if the darkest moments were showing you something deep?

What if the downest of days were there to help you see what you couldn't otherwise see?

What if challenges came your way as a gift?

What if every challenge was for you?

But in the moment, all you can do is feel mad, frustrated, and down on yourself.

What if every gray day was a chance to rest, a chance to reset?

What if the spaces around you spoke to you?

What if you spent all your days upset at the world and you missed the messages?

What if the people you passed, the strangers who walked by, the workers on the street, all had a message...

But there you were, feeling bad and sad and miserable, missing it?

What if you looked and saw another world?

What if the mural of your life came alive?

What if everything that happens in your life is to wake you up?

What if every being is here to remind you?

What if the wagging tails and the disruption in your world are to show you something more special than you can receive when you're worried and scared?

What if the problems are not problems at all, but messages?

What if every being in your life is there to remind you of your soul?

What if, when you settle down to comfort yourself, it's in that moment that you feel your soul nudge you...

To tell you that all around you there are sweet and loving things to remind you of the world that's here for you?

What if, in the moment just before you say, "good night," you feel a special blessing?

What if your ice cream bowl is sweet to remind you to savor it all?

What if your pillows are angel wings sent to comfort you?

What if, just when you venture out, just when you're ready to see, raindrops come your way?

What if you need to see differently?

What if the drops of rain are blessings that help you change your route or put on that special coat?

What if every leaf and branch along your way is there to protect you, like an outstretched army of angels?

What if your "oops" is a moment for an angel to show up in person?

What if a spill or a mess helps you see others jump into action to help you?

What if your "bad luck" is an opening to receive?

What if you never did receive your angels?

What if bad luck is what angels are here for?

What if you're surrounded by helpers and your needs are their purpose?

The magic is what they are here for.

What if you missed all the magic?

What if you heard the angels guiding the way and pushing you forward, in a direction you might not find on your own?

What if every moment with a friend is a light from an angel?

What if even hard rocks are safe places to rest?

What if our friends could hold our hearts and help change them into stars?

What if we could reach out and light up another, and be their angel?

What if we could all just stop and see all beings as beams of love, of beautiful energy?

What if the whole world is pulsing with potential and it is our life's work to realize it?

What if those in your path are looking at something other than the rain?

What if rainbows are a chance to understand how life gives us light and fun, just when we lose hope?

What if every dimension of our world speaks to us in everyday happenings to show us our soul?

What if the "rain" in our lives washes the grime and dirt away to show us the beauty underneath?

What if we just need to look at it all differently?

What if it were that easy?

What if we are opening the beauty and the light by how we feel?

What if our words and feelings are what imprison or free us?

What if we knew the exact moment to free our soul?

What if each moment is a **chance** to free our soul?

What if we could practice freeing our soul by smiling at children?

What if we could dance in our hearts like they play?

What if every child in the world is a chance to see how our soul truly wants to live?

What if we could capture the light in our words?

What if we could make that light bigger by writing it all down?

What if we saw the words on the page bounce around and play?

If our words were the difference between writing thoughts and the voice of our soul...

If our feelings came alive in our hearts to dance in front of our eyes...

What if we saw it all each morning to start our blessed day?

What if we took our bright souls everywhere we went?

What if, because of our souls, so bright and full, we made the world better, everywhere?

What if we walked around and lived as brightly as all the angels?

What if those in our path saw us as soul light?

What if our smile brightened them?

What if we felt the light inside come alive?

What if each and every moment was exactly what a stranger or a friend needed?

What if you are special in a deep way?

What if small tasks and every day events brightened you even more?

What if your specialness was felt in every way, deep inside?

What if you knew, as surely as the sun, that your soul is special?

What if you know it now, so deep that it's never a question?

What if you know your soul is humming the words to a new song?

What if your special place on the earth is exactly where you are now?

What if right here is all there is?

What if it's YOU?

The very one you have been wanting to help you, the very one you've sought...

What if she's YOU?

What if the emptiness and doubt you feel can be filled by your own soul?

It's you...

You are the one, made specially to brighten your own soul!

What if even the buildings come alive and everything around you is pulsing **because** of YOU?

What if all you have to do is be a bigger soul?

What if the workers are waiting and the animals know how special your soul is, and they're waiting for you to see?

WHAT if...

Every moment of your life is a time to feel the WOW, every breath a special energy to bring it all to life?

What if everyone you meet is for you and you for them?

What if...

It's all connected and pulsing so we can all mend.

It's all one so we can experience oneness?

What if?

What a great life to know you are blessed in each moment.

What a great awakening to know your fears brought you closer to your soul.

What an amazing world that all the world is a buzz and one with souls.

What an amazing world of potential to shine billions of souls at the same time.

Pass it around, will you? That very bright you...

What if YOUR SOUL is exactly what the world needs right now?

Would you shine for us, please? Would you be one with us?

Bios

Writer:

Mo Faul, Coach Mo to her clients, spent over 30 years learning the ropes of corporate survival and success as she balanced it with the spiritual ambition of wanting to know herself and how she best fit into the world. Breast cancer sidelined her long enough to see that her soul was aching to grow and be seen. Returning to work as a soulful executive, she gained insight into what is missing for many humans: finding meaning in life. A striking experience of divine connection during the COVID-19 pandemic brought this story to her. Her clients and fans are eager to be inspired by this story, their tale of awakening.

Illustrator:

Laura Nielsen found her soul and realized the world is helping her be her in working with Coach Mo Faul. One deep coaching session revealed to Laura and Coach Mo a beautiful artist inside Laura's professional self. Moved to witness Laura's talent, when Mo needed an illustrator to tell her story, she asked Laura to dive in. Laura has developed as an artist as she has managed her soul's growth and her family through the great awakening on the planet and in her soul. Laura resides outside Knoxville, TN with her husband, family, and soulful dogs.

CPSIA information can be obtained
at www.ICGtesting.com
Printed in the USA
BVHW021638180422
633854BV00002B/3